The Book of Idle Pleasures

The Book of Idle Pleasures

Edited by

Tom Hodgkinson

&

Dan Kieran

Illustrated by Ged Wells

**Andrews McMeel
Publishing, LLC**

Kansas City • Sydney • London

The Book of Idle Pleasures copyright © 2010 by Tom Hodgkinson,
Dan Kieran, and Ged Wells. All rights reserved. Printed in China.
No part of this book may be used or reproduced in any manner
whatsoever without written permission except in the case of re-
prints in the context of reviews. For information, write Andrews
McMeel Publishing, LLC, an Andrews McMeel Universal company, 1130 Walnut Street, Kansas City, Missouri 64106.

10 11 12 13 14 SDB 10 9 8 7 6 5 4 3 2 1

ISBN-13: 978-0-7407-8508-5
ISBN-10: 0-7407-8508-7

Library of Congress Control Number: 2009940829

First published in Great Britain by Ebury Press, an imprint of
Ebury Publishing, a Random House Group company

Tom Hodgkinson, Dan Kieran, and Ged Wells have asserted their
rights to be identified as the authors of this work.

ATTENTION: SCHOOLS AND BUSINESSES
Andrews McMeel books are available at quantity discounts with
bulk purchase for educational, business, or sales promotional
use. For information, please write to: Special Sales Department,
Andrews McMeel Publishing, LLC, 1130 Walnut Street, Kansas
City, Missouri 64106.

Introduction

Life admits not of delays; when pleasure
can be had, it is fit to catch it.
– Dr. Johnson

It is the purpose of this book to prove that the
best things in life really are free. For the last two
centuries or so, we in the West have labored
under the delusion that fun is a costly business.
We work hard doing things we don't enjoy in
order to make money to spend on doing things
that we do enjoy. Well, the idle pleasure helps us
to escape all of that costly confusion and disap-
pointment. The idle pleasure helps us elegantly
to sidestep all the commotion and bustle and
stress of the work-hard, shop-hard world, and
enter a world of joy and freedom. And indulging
in pleasure for its own sake may be a rebellious
act, which tends to add a certain savor. Since

Martin Luther, and later the fun-hating Puritans, the Reformed Church has attacked pleasure as being irrelevant to the serious business of salvation and making money. Pleasure, particularly if not paid for, is supremely useless. It does not contribute to the growth of the economy. "Illicit pleasures are banned until they become profitable," remarks the Belgian philosopher Raoul Vaneigem in *The Book of Pleasures*. He also writes: "I want to fight for more fun, not less pain."

Idle pleasure is about self-management, freedom, independence. When we take a guilt-free nap under the trees in the park in summer, we are reclaiming our right to live how we choose. When we take a stroll at a deliberately slow pace through the city, and merely observe the currents of life without submitting to the urge to shop, we are making an enjoyable protest against the work-and-consume society.

Idle pleasure can also reconnect us with nature. Man's great program over the last two or three hundred years has been to reject those parts of nature that we don't like. Hence air-conditioning, central gas heating, concrete, motorcars, and Internet social networking Web sites. All of these man-made constructions attempt to sidestep messy nature. They are attempts to create a brave new world where the aging process can be slowed down and mud and cold don't exist.

But idlers love nature. It costs nothing, and it's therapeutic. Something as simple as skipping a stone on a rocky beach brings us back down to earth. No one has had to buy the stone, or rent the water, or go to a stone-skipping class. There are enough stones to go around. In fact, the idea for this book came when Ged Wells and I were sitting in Woody Bay, the nearest beach to where I live, and reflecting on the fact that nature provides its stuff for free, whereas man-made pleasures are very expensive. We'd noticed also that far from any retail outlet, the children didn't fight or whine or ask us to buy them stuff: there was plenty of sea and sand for everyone so there was no need to compete.

Idle pleasure, too, is supremely eco-friendly. There is nothing less harmful to the environment than doing nothing. Lying in a field and staring at the sky may be a planet-healing act. It is man's interfering and tragic need for action that has caused the gluttonous draining of the earth's oil and gas.

We need to take a look at the old ways. Too often, anyone who looks to history for ideas for living today is labeled as romantic or nostalgic.

But I would argue that to do the opposite, which is to believe in the future, is completely irrational. The future hasn't happened yet and therefore is a mere abstraction. And does an accumulation of labor-saving gadgets really save labor? Don't all those machines, designed to banish unpleasant toil, actually increase our workload, since we expect ourselves, in the words of the modern marketeer, to "do more"? But the old idea of making your own fun, using your own creativity and imagination rather than paying someone else to do it for you, is, I think, a sensible approach. And what could be simpler and more enjoyable than leaning on a gate? Truly the bare necessities of life will come to you.

In a world of nonstop toil and stress and bother, the idle pleasure can help us to live again, to enjoy ourselves, to indulge our built-in love of nature and sensuality and conviviality, without breaking our backs, or the bank. So let's throw off the shackles of modern life and embrace pleasure. It's the real thing.

TOM HODGKINSON
North Devon
February 2008

Contents

The Pleasures ...

Taking a Bath

In a world of "power showers" and invigorating pick-me-up gel products for the modern striver, it's good to remember the simple pleasures of a long, relaxing bath, preferably taken at eleven a.m. when everyone else is toiling in the mills and you have phoned in sick. Follow the medieval tradition and fill your bath with spices and rose petals. Invite your lover to join you. Linger in the bath too long and add hot water by twisting the taps with your feet, because you are too lazy to sit up and use your hands. Lie there and stare at the ceiling, almost — but not quite — drifting into the land of Nod, perfectly at ease, as the steam rises around you and the workaday world recedes into the realm of unimportance.

TH

Poking the Fire

Once you've got a roaring fire going, indulge yourself in the simple pleasure of giving it a good poke. The poker is not just there to help revive a dying fire. It is best used when the flames are threatening to set fire to the chimney and you are having difficulty getting close enough to the grate to place it amid the burning embers. Use it then to swiftly reposition any lumps of coal that are slightly out of position or marginally off-center, fashioning a red-hot cradle for the final touch, a nice, dry evergreen log. Preferably with a dusting of frost, ice, or snow still on it, as this damp coating will help add a pleasant variety to the smoke coming from the conflagration and may also provide a satisfying hissing sound. Before you lean back in the cozy armchair to take another long pull on that delicious twenty-five-year-old malt whisky that you have been saving for just such a moment, thrust the poker into the heart of the fire and leave it there. After a few minutes the poker will be red-hot; remove it from the fire and plunge it into a bucket of cold water. Now enjoy the shuddering sensation as it immediately cools and acrid fumes rise from the bucket.

JS

Slouching

Ninety-five percent of communication is non-verbal and your body has a language all of its own. "Stop slouching!" cried your mother and your teacher, but slouching is the posture of calm rebellion. It's a leisurely thumbing of the nose to the productive classes. It has its down-sides, though, and is cited as a cause of decreased alertness and varicose veins — making it undoubtedly the smoking of seating.

DK

Leaf Catching

The first autumn leaves are beginning to flutter down around my house, signaling the start of a traditional family ritual. To ensure good luck for the next twelve months it is important that, when the autumn winds are blowing, we go outside and catch — or try to catch — twelve falling leaves. It sounds easy, but twisting, spiraling, flying leaves are not easy to snatch out of the air. And the competition for extra-colorful or nice-shaped specimens can be fierce when a flurry of them whiz past, making for excellent and sometimes quite violent sport.

CY

The Balcony

A good balcony is an essential ingredient for a day of languor. It can be on the eighteenth floor of a high-rise, where you water the window box of daisies, sit on a deck chair with a bottle of beer, and consider the intricate, interwoven stories of the city. It can be on the third floor of a condo in Florida, with the ocean below waiting for you to make up your mind, as you stumble around in front of the barbecue, gripping a bottle of red wine by the neck. It can be on the fourth floor of your office, site of clandestine joints, snatched sexual liaisons, and an exultation of indifference toward that damned job. Wherever you find your balcony, savor its essential pleasure — half inside, half outside. Like the hokey-pokey, you have one foot in the world, and one foot out.

MDA

Waiting for the Tea to Brew

Enforced idleness is a rare treat. Those brief moments in life where for one reason or another you are forced to just stop and think. In waiting rooms, in line, for example, or even just sitting on a train. Waiting for the tea to brew is one of such moments. It doesn't offer enough time to "do" anything else so you just have to sit and wait, salivating at the prospect of your golden brew. If you do attempt to do anything in the time it takes tea to brew, you always take too long or too short a time to do it, leaving the tea too strong or too weak. The teapot is fully aware of this fact. The only way to gauge the time perfectly is to sit, do nothing, and watch. Only by handing over your full attention to the pot will you be able to truly relish the taste when the moment comes.

DK

13

Messing About in Boats

There's nothing quite like messing around in boats. From Ratty and his chums to Jerome K. Jerome's *Three Men in a Boat*, the daydreaming enemies of work have always sought solace in the slowed-down worlds of our rivers and canals. There can be no better way to drift off into peaceful reveries than lying in a drifting boat, opening one's eyes to see a patch of sky, a cloud, slow-moving treetops. Like so many idle pleasures, boating is a way to legitimize doing nothing. There is plenty to occupy one-self with — locks, preparing food, steering the boat — but in reality you are doing nothing of any use to anyone. Which is wonderful. Boating doesn't get you anywhere — it would always be quicker to go by car. The pleasure lies in the moment.

TH

Tree Houses

Originally designed as a shelter to keep people above the deadly hazards to be found on the floor of subtropical rainforests, today they take us back to a world of slingshots and gumballs, and shelter childhoods from the prying mania of modern parenting. Built from any old bits of crap found in hedges, floorboards from skiffs, salvaged driftwood, or storm-damaged trees, there is only one rule when it comes to construction. Make it large and strong enough to hold ten children while making it look small and weak enough to dissuade any adventurous adults from venturing up too high. Avoid at all costs buying new lumber from the superstore. Tree houses should be flawed, beautiful, scruffy, and unique.

DK

Strolling through the City

In nineteenth-century Paris, there was a type
of man known as the *flâneur*. He was a sort
of strolling dandy, a work-shunning poet,
who ambled through the city, lingering in
the arcades, lolling on benches, and making
observations. Some of the most extreme
flâneurs used to take a tortoise on their walks,
because they liked to let the tortoise set the
pace. You can be a modern-day *flâneur* in your
own town: just set out from your front door
and make a deliberate attempt to walk slowly.
It will seem unnatural at first, but that is only
because you are starting to overcome years of
A-to-B speed-walking conditioning. Soon the
slower pace will become more habitual, and you
will take great pleasure in the world of limitless
wonder that ambling opens up to you.

TH

Procrastinating

Jerome K. Jerome once wrote, "Idleness, like kisses, to be sweet must be stolen," and thus we enter the blissful world of procrastination. When else are those few extra minutes in bed so utterly delicious than when you should really already be on your way to work? I suppose you could start your homework right now and then have a day off before you have to hand it in, but how much better to have that day off now before you've even started any work at all. Steal back your time from those troublesome errands and wallow in it, savoring every second. I've certainly never found the expanded-edition boxed set of the *Lord of the Rings* trilogy quite as alluring as I did when the deadline for this very book approached. But it takes dedication to learn how to procrastinate properly. All deadlines must still be met, or the theft of time loses its effect. In fact, the slogan on every workplace up and down the land should be just that: "Minimum effort, maximum effect!"

DK

Letting the Weeds Grow

Thanks to our Puritan forefathers, we have a very strict and antinature view of gardening. Weeds must be blasted with sprays. Bugs likewise. Everything must be neat and in straight lines. But do you see a straight line in nature? Surely we should be kinder to the weeds and let them grow — in moderation — alongside the flowers and fruits that we have planted. It is said that a weed is simply a flower in the wrong place. And weeds are free. "If people would only look at the weeds in their gardens," says the nature writer Robin Page, "they would see that they already have many free and attractive flowers." And what would life be without some wild places? As Gerard Manley Hopkins puts it:

> *What would the world be, once bereft*
> *Of wet and wildness? Let them be left,*
> *Oh let them be left, wildness and wet*
> *Long live the weeds and wilderness yet.*

TH

The Deck Chair

Who does not love a deck chair? Wittgenstein did. It was the only item of furniture he allowed in his study at Trinity, Cambridge, supposedly a testament to his asceticism. I instead saw it as the ideal solution to the problem of how to maneuver something comfy to sit on up the narrow stairs to my study. But that the greatest philosopher of the twentieth century saw in the deck chair a sufficiency of design and purpose should say something about the perfect utility of this furniture item. Imagine this: a chair so comfy you can sleep in it, which can be carried when not in use. The deck chair symbolizes ad hoc leisure, snatched naps, impromptu basking. It speaks to us of the sea, wherever it is; in my study, relaxing in it, I hear the faint calling of gulls, and even, in deeper reverie, the vanished days of the ocean liners whence it got its name. Somewhere, a bell rings; it is time to rise, and dress for dinner at the captain's table.

NL

Taking a Nap

Of all the free pleasures out there for the taking, the nap is the easiest and the most satisfying. Traditionally taken at noon or the sixth hour — hence the word *siesta* — in order to sleep through the visits of the noonday demons, the postlunch doze is an everyday reality for those living in less work-obsessed countries. It's a criminal shame that in Northern Europe and the United States naps must be taken secretly and guiltily; after all, they are the most natural thing in the world. It is crazy to work for eight hours or more at a stretch without any sleep. We should take a pillow wherever we go. We need to find corners for dozing, in the church or in the park. A nap every day will do the work of a million vitamin supplements and energy capsules. Gentle, sweet, care-charming sleep, medicine for the weary soul!

TH

Déjà Vu

There are many theories as to what causes déjà vu. One holds that our "spirit" can actually travel faster in time than our earthbound bodies so it charges off into the future from time to time for reasons we can't explain. Another claims that it's because we are reincarnated and old memories from past lives are seeping through into our current consciousness. And then there's the parallel universe theory that suggests our lives are always splitting off into different directions whenever we make big decisions and that at the point of experiencing déjà vu we are connecting with these parallel worlds.

All of which rather ignores the actual sensation of déjà vu that is simply joyous and mesmerizing regardless of what it actually is. Déjà vu experiences stay with us, too, logging themselves into our memory banks, where they can be withdrawn whenever those "déjà vu" conversations occur, usually over a few glasses of wine late at night. As it happens, I have a déjà vu theory of my own. I think it's our brains rebooting — a neurological safety mechanism designed to clear the decks of our consciousness and leave us fresh and awake.

DK

The Public Bench

Which genius invented the public bench? In our increasingly controlled, targeted, and digitized world, the wooden public bench is a haven of freedom in the middle of the city. On the bench you can read, doze, eat your sandwich, meditate, and reflect on the vanity of human wishes. The town elders can sit on the bench and watch the world pass by. Mothers with their babies can leaf through a thin volume of verse while the little ones sleep. Clandestine meetings can be held on the bench, and confidences exchanged without fear of surveillance. The bench offers conviviality, solitude, and comfort. All at a cost of not a cent.

TH

31

Dog Walking

As Walt Whitman wrote, you really have to get
outside to see beauty and to see poetry: "The
passionate tenacity of hunters, woodmen, early
risers, cultivators of gardens and orchards and
fields . . . seafaring persons, drivers of horses,
their passion for light and the open air,—all is
an old unvaried sign of the failing perception
of beauty, and of a residence of the poetic in
outdoor people." Because a dog has to walk,
owning a dog forces you to leave the fireside and
breathe in some cold, bracing air. And the joy
of the animal as it sniffs and bounds and plays,
endlessly curious and always in the moment,
transmits itself to the owner, and you feel real
joy, too. And how pleasant it is to return to the
fireside after having breathed your fill of outdoor
air, and watch tired doggie curl up and go to
sleep.

TH

The Beach

Choose a beach with no shops or ice cream vendors or cafés or parking lots, and you'll find that everyone is happy. Parents can read or paddle; kids can discover their own creativity through that fantastic modeling material, wet sand. There will be no arguments over pebbles because there are always enough pebbles to go around. Unlike the world of consumer products, nature is bountiful and provides plenty for everyone, meaning there is no room for fighting. You can choose to swim or to stare at the ocean or to play in the rock-pools and catch shrimp. You can eat your sandwiches or grill some fish on a make-shift barbecue: a world of ease is there for the taking.

TH

Just Looking

It used to be called browsing. But browsing implied a freedom to roam with no obligation to buy. "Just looking" is different. Your entry into the shop has aroused expectation in the Armani-clad assistant. You are his ticket to a sale, an extension of the brand. A well-placed "just looking" shifts the power balance. Pick some things up and put them back down again. Shop rents are so high that every minute you're "just looking" you're also shoplifting — stealing attention, space, and valuable "brand-time." You are a flâneur dwelling within the flow of the shop but individually unchallenged. Everyone else is a consumer. You're "just looking."

AM

Melancholy

In a world where we are accustomed to attacking depression without mercy with heavy-duty mood-leveling potions such as Ativan and Prozac, it is easy to forget that there can be a pleasure in melancholic brooding. You can fancy yourself to be a Romantic poet, wandering in the groves and summoning rhymes to describe your misery. In that great seventeenth-century self-help book, *The Anatomy of Melancholy*, Robert Burton writes: "A most incomparable delight it is to melancholize, and build castles in the air, to go smiling to themselves, acting an infinite variety of parts." And Burton should know; after all, he did write the book on it.

TH

Walking with Toddlers

Toddlers don't understand the concept of walking as a function. For them it is a chance just to amble about while staring at bricks and clumps of earth and marveling at how they came to be on the pavement. They double back, walk sideways, and often simply stop walking altogether before staring attentively up into the sky. Instead of getting cross and trying to hurry them on, embrace the way they follow one impulse of curiosity after another. Toddlers are the masters of instinct. Once you have rejected your agitated impulses that seem intent on driving you on and on, you will discover what it truly means to be relaxed. At first this process may be frustrating for a hassled adult, but once you have abandoned the hope of being somewhere at a specific time, you will find yourself reveling in a state of childlike torpor.

While you're following this nobler means of perambulation, the world around you will begin to morph into a more magical place. Sticks you would have otherwise trampled on turn into the staffs and swords that swoosh through the air to the echo of brave, long-forgotten heroes.

DK

Singing

Before the age of the radio and iPod, we all used to sing, all of us, all day long. If you walked down the street in Florence in 1350, you would hear every craftsperson and trader bellowing out songs both secular and divine, folk songs, courtly love songs, lyrics by Dante. The gloom of the late Puritan age has killed much of this joyful expression. But it lingers still, on the building site or in the garage. So sing again! Sing once more, as we used to in the old days!

TH

Sunbeams

In a daze, you climb down the stairs on a
summer morning. All the curtains in the room
below are closed except one. A sunbeam cuts
through the darkness and onto the blue carpet —
dust flecked in its refracting light. Your bare
feet lead you to its edge. You dip your toe in
the warmth before submerging your entire foot.
A line of glowing light draws itself across your
ankle, restoring you with its gentle affection.
Gradually you get on your knees and immerse
yourself into the light completely. You curl up in
a ball and go back to sleep.

DK

Sticking Matchsticks into Vegetables to Make Vegetable Aliens

Who needs toy superstores and Web sites when you can make your own toys for nothing? Just take a zucchini, a potato, or a turnip and stick matches into it for arms and legs. Push the matches right in so only the head is showing— and hey presto, you've got eyes. Laugh at your alien and then laugh heartily at yourself. What a joy it is to be a fool.

TH

Looking at Maps

What is it about maps and globes that seems to require our undivided attention? I've spent hours looking at maps of places I will never see and maps so old that they are a record of nothing but the faintest glow of the past. Perhaps they turn us into gods, letting us look down at the insignificant drones that occupy the earth. Or maybe they simply feed off our hunger to go off into the unknown. Venturing off to places where people don't chain themselves to tedious jobs and absurd financial debts but places of imagination, mystery, and freedom.

Having said that, map origami can be a bit of a bore when you try to recontain the huge billboard of paper back in the precise predetermined folds, but then again I quite like the idea that they don't want to be put away. Perhaps they're just trying to tell us something.

DK

Sowing Seeds

Whether you scatter seeds, or dig little holes for them, or space them carefully in a shallow trench, the act of putting seeds into earth is immensely refreshing and enjoyable. It helps us to reconnect with the earth, not such an easy task these days, as we live in a world that has conciously tried to remove us from the soil. In sowing seeds, you allow a simple childlike wonder to overtake you. First, there is the huge variety of shapes and sizes. Then there is the fact that from these tiny seeds, vegetables and flowers will grow, which themselves will bring pleasure and sustenance.

TH

Hanging Out the Laundry

Household chores are one of the few occasions when our brains get to relax while our bodies take care of something mundane. Providing you only have to do your share of household chores, rather than all of them, they can become a simple pleasure in themselves. Take hanging laundry out on the clothesline. First you collect the sodden garments from the washing machine and carry them outside in one of those pleasant little baskets. Then you get the satisfying "thwack" of shaking and uncrumpling pairs of trousers and tangled sweaters and finally you get to reach out for the clothespins. The humble clothespin—such simple and wondrous design. Up on the line your damp clothes go to be buffeted by the breeze. Socks are arranged in pairs where possible. Your lover's undergarments allow you a moment of lascivious reflection and go side by side in turn. Then you get to your own underwear and immediately resolve to chuck out some of the more threadbare graying items. Finally you collect the bag of clothespins and throw it with a clunk into your now empty basket and stroll contentedly back inside.

DK

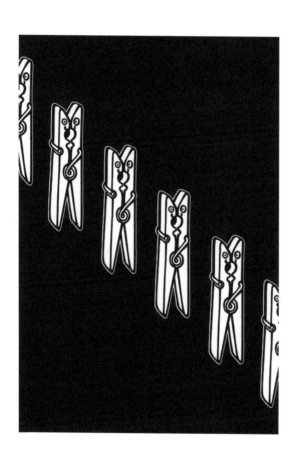

53

Being Ill

Far from being a drag, being ill can offer its own bittersweet pleasures. First, there is the very welcome break from work and the opportunity to spend three days in bed. While in bed, you can do what you want. You eat fruit and drink delicious spicy hot drinks. You read *Sherlock Holmes* and David Sedaris. You drift into dreamland and enjoy that delectable realm that lies between wakefulness and sleep. Thanks precisely to your physical lack of get-up-and-go, you can unwind yourself from the taut, stressful working world that has riddled your body with infection. Let the relaxed pieces of your soul wallow and repair themselves while you stare blindly at the black-and-white movies of daytime TV or submit to the freewheeling eddies of your feverish subconscious.

TH

Sleeping in Your Clothes

After a busy day you find yourself lying on the
sofa drifting off into a hypnagogic state in front
of a muttering TV screen. Your brain is just
awake enough to inform you that at this point
you should really get up, brush your teeth,
wash your face, get undressed, and loll into bed.
However, if you do get up, brush your teeth,
wash your face, and get undressed, then by
the time you are ready to loll into bed, you'll
be wide awake again and the delightful spell
will have broken. So instead, revel freely in the
moment that sleep threatens to envelop you. The
enchantment in nodding off and then nodding
awake a few minutes later is like a gentle roller
coaster that goes slowly enough to be thrilling
while managing to avoid the unpleasantness of
any theme park sensations. Remain motionless,
allow your mind to wander off, and enjoy the
thrill of sleeping in your clothes. Leave the TV
warbling to itself and luxuriate in the sensation
of stalking slumber. When you wake in the small
hours with a slight chill, you can sleepwalk to
your bedroom before your comforter greedily
swallows you whole.

DK

Arranging Records

(This particular pleasure is nontransferable to other media with
the exception of books. Anyone attempting to arrange CDs or
MP3 audio files will be sorely disappointed.)

Some prefer the obvious merits of alphabetization,
musical genre, or the month and year of release,
but surely more radical means of classification are
available. I knew a man once who arranged his
records according to Pantone reference, giving
his lounge a literal rainbow of music along his
far wall for visitors to peruse. The delight of an
arrangement that is unpredictable is, things that
are otherwise overlooked get the chance to stand
out from the crowd. Then there are new unlikely
friendships that might emerge. When else might
you consider the parallels between a Prince guitar
masterpiece and the latest offering from Metallica?
Who knows where the next mix tape might lead?

Books can benefit from the exercise of misar-
rangement on your shelves, too. It's hard for
Agatha Christie to stand out when she always has
to sit next to Raymond Chandler. Or for Charles
Darwin to have to constantly suffer his latest toady
Richard Dawkins. Unless your shelves are always
jumbled, in which case a reunion might just be in
order, or a reorder, depending on your mood.

DK

Caves

By a lake in a clutch of trees, a hunk of rock
seems out of place and unfamiliar. You break
from the path and head toward it, pondering,
What is this rambling pile of stone? The soft
white exterior grows up from a bed of flint and
you drag your hand across it while traversing the
grass that leads up to its edge. Aha! Around the
back an opening appears — just large enough to
scrape through with the possibility of leaving a
tear in your clothes. Once you've scraped your
way inside, your eyes tighten and you hear the
sound of a "drip, drip, drip, drip." Moss has
long since claimed the insides of this old ice-
house, hewn from alien stone and the fragments
of ancient shells. The floor falls down below you
in makeshift steps. Bracken creeps through the
cracks here and there, but this time machine of
nature is untouched, offering a haven from the
ills of the world. You creep out again and grin —
pondering whether it will still exist when you
return. For all caves must be shared.

DK

Face-Pulling Competitions

Face-pulling was the medieval word for gurning, and it's actually a more expressive term.

Everyone in the room has to pull the most ghoulish face they can. Take a record, if you like, with Polaroid film or a digital camera. The winner is the one who manages the most terrifying or comical expression. Look at medieval cathedrals for inspiration.

TH

Not Opening Letters

A handwritten envelope landing on your mat is a rare treat. All we seem to get nowadays are bills and unwanted junk mail (corporate stalking by another name). There's something terribly frightening about official-looking mail. British comedian Peter Cook was renowned for having mountains of unopened letters behind his front door. The fear of not knowing what such envelopes contain, and where the information inside them could lead you, is best dealt with by ignoring them completely. Whenever I search through old drawers, I find reams of unopened envelopes from official-sounding institutions, some of which date back to the previous millennium. Did completely ignoring them affect me? Not in the slightest. Because when it's really urgent, you will always receive a phone call. And if money is involved, someone will always get in touch before the heavies are called in, and then you can pay what you owe over the phone. So ignore these envelopes of terror. Strip them of their power and sling them all, unopened, where they belong — in the trash.

DK

Tree Climbing

Why do we need to pay to go to hellish anti-
septic odor-free plastic kids' playgrounds, when
trees are all around us for climbing? Trees,
which are all different, all unique, all magical,
are there for the taking, for the climbing, for the
sitting in, for the smelling. Become like a bird.

                                                    TH

Sneering

Look at that guy; does he think he looks nice?
Doesn't he have a mirror? And what about
him? Small-time middle-of-the-litter function-
ary, tabloid reader, suburban voyeur, scared of
everything, bitter, pity his poor wife, the frigid
hag. Silly old fool, stupid young idiot, if you
can't drive, get off the road, madam, look at that
jerk, funny how Audis have replaced BMWs as
the pricks' car of choice, my God, if that's what
you put in your supermarket cart, madam, no
wonder you're so fat.

Sneering. Nothing like it. Walk through the
streets at dusk. Everything is sneer worthy.
Dinner party in a McMansion, glimpsed through
vulgar interior-designed curtains? No insight,
boring losers. Man on his own watching TV in
his vest? Johnny no-friends and no wonder; by
midnight he'll be on a porno line somewhere,
Busty Samantha. People at a bus stop: fools. Man
standing looking at them with a sneer on his
"face": fool, loser, boring, no insight, Johnny
no-friends, sod. Okay. Let's leave it there.

MB

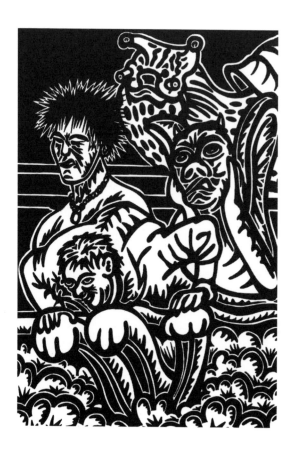

Reading Poetry

It's a forgotten pleasure in our rushed days, to
leaf through a slim volume of verse, perhaps
while riding the bus or when resting by a tree
in the city park. Everyone should keep a book of
poetry about their person. Even to read four lines
of Keats while waiting for a friend will enrich
your day. Here is Keats, for example, on the
pleasures of red wine:

> O for a draught of vintage! that hath been
> Cool'd a long age in the deep-delvèd earth,
> Tasting of Flora and the country-green,
> Dance, and Provençal song, and sunburnt mirth!

What a phrasemaker he was! Words well chosen
can fill your heart with joy. Reject the empty
clatter of pulp fiction and keep a book of poetry
on your person at all times.

TH

Squishing Bread

There are few more appropriate ways to show your appreciation of the humble loaf than by squishing it. That unmistakable sensation beneath your fingers as you press down — first the gentle resistance of the crust, and then the euphoric give of the doughy insides.

And yet each loaf is different. The bread aisle sings out as you walk past, rows of starchy sirens longing for your attention. All plastic pap, but squishable nonetheless. You come out of the aisle, euphoric, and what lies before you but the bakery! Truly the Bonnaroo of the bread-squishing world, the place where all the freaks come out to play. Loaves, rolls, ciabattas, bagels, baguettes — with their strange, foreign textures, they give no quarter and take no prisoners. Sophisticated Europeans or unrefined bumpkins, they offer the greatest challenge to the recreational squisher, but the greatest rewards, too.

EC

Perusing the Sky Mall Catalog

The absurd labor-saving devices lovingly
pictured and described in Sky Mall catalogs
are strangely seductive. How often have we
nonchalantly picked one up, expecting to swiftly
stuff it back into the seat pocket, and then found
ourselves utterly enthralled? Even the call of
our Sudoku puzzles has no effect: we sit rapt,
unable to move. The pleasure is compounded by
the knowledge that we will never in a million
years actually fork out for an air ionizer, electric
translator, Corby trouser press, water purifier,
towel warmer, or mechanical grasper. No — the
pleasure lies in laughing at the follies and
vanities of man's silly little ideas.

TH

Sleeping Outside

Sleeping with the worms comes to us all in the end, so doing it when you are very much alive is an alluring experience. Whether in a wood next to a campfire with friends or in your garden on a sticky summer's night, the nocturnal rumblings of the twilight world are ideal sleeping companions. For the best effect, however, lie on the grass covered by an old blanket at midnight in mid-August to look for the Perseids shower — an annual display of meteors that fill the summer sky with shooting stars. Grab friends and family and lie down together, like spokes on a wheel with your heads in the center, and gasp and whoop in delight as the heavens burst into life.

DK

Dreaming

Dreamland is the original cyberspace, our own built-in spiritual virtual reality. Our dreams take us into other worlds, alternative realities that help us make sense of day-to-day life. Dreaming is a connection to our unconscious, to our selves. It is to be treasured. And, as Debbie Harry wisely reminds us, it's free. Isn't it extraordinary that an activity that takes up so much of our lives is so often relegated into the realm of unimportance? We are based on dreams; they are at our center. Listen to them.

TH

Telling Stories

Here is another art that has been lost as a result of a surfeit of books, story tapes, DVDs, videos, Web sites, and television programs — all of which delegate the act of telling stories to an outside "expert." But reading aloud to one another in the evenings, not just to the children but to other adults, is supremely enjoyable. It is also vastly preferable to television, in that you can choose what you read rather than meekly submitting to the choice of the schedulers. And making up your own stories is surprisingly easy, and children appear to take more delight in fresh and spontaneous tales than in the ones you read from a book.

TH

Feeling the Wind in Your Hair

The peak of the cliff sits tantalizingly close. Your hands rest on your knees as you gasp, willing more oxygen into your lungs. You look back with pride down the way you've come. Just a little farther and you'll be there. Your energy now partially restored, you step on and on. The light wind lifts the closer you get to the peak. A plateau soon falls away abruptly down to the sea, and the sweeping air collects and whips into your face. The view is sublime but the payoff comes as you stand — arms stretched wide in triumph — with your eyes closed as the raging wind buffets your face. This wind, collected and grown above oceans, flitting and crashing its way across the waves, finally reaches the shore and clasps itself around you in a fleeting embrace. The crack of its passing meets your ears and slowly it absorbs you — a streaming current of air caressing your rejoicing face.

DK

Staring

You're inside; the world is outside. Staring through the window offers thinkers and dreamers unparalleled opportunities to ruminate, and, in the best tradition of the pathetic fallacy, the sights beyond the glass will always reflect our mood. If we are feeling bright and optimistic, the birds will be singing and the children playing. If we're feeling miserable and blue, then it will be raining and the trees will be bare. Window-starers, however, usually find that it is raining and the trees are bare. There is something about staring through a window that is suited to melancholic temperaments. It is only through steady application to window staring that we will manage to transform it from a sad exercise into a positive one.

TH

The Bathrobe

There is no more apt uniform of sloth than the bathrobe. Merely owning one is a sign of hope. A signal of slovenly intent. Bathrobes accompany the state of doing nothing, but what are you actually doing when you're doing nothing? Thinking, that's what you're doing. Society fears the population with time to think. Populations like that have been known to change things. This is why the bathrobe is the true uniform of revolution. In some far distant point in the future, women and men will marvel at the day the seats of global power were finally overwhelmed — by an army of people in bathrobes.

DK

A Pack of Cards

In a world of Nintendo Wiis and DSs, of Sony
PlayStations and a myriad of more costly fun
machines that are destined to hit the garbage
within two years, it's well to remember the
low-cost miracle of the pack of cards. Here is a
piece of entertainment that is portable, requires
no batteries or power source, and never crashes.
You need to buy no additional extras for it. It
offers a thousand games, from easy kids' games
to sophisticated and complex adult games. You
can play one-player games with it and ease the
passage of time. You can do tricks with it; you
can amuse and amaze. A pack of cards is a thing
of beauty in itself: in its queens and kings, jacks
and jokers, an old courtly world is remembered,
a world of chivalry and knightly values.

TH

Chatting with the Mail Carrier

Beware the World Wide Web and shun the dastardly Internet. Why allow yourself to be advertised at by greedy cynics on ad-filled social networking Web sites when you can talk to the mail carrier for free every day? Or the green-grocer or the butcher, for that matter. The com-modification of human interaction has been one of the worst crimes of the digital age. We do not need Web pages designed to sell us things to talk to other human beings. Or what about that amazing invention I heard about the other day? It enables you to speak to someone on the OTHER SIDE OF THE WORLD whenever you like and doesn't sneak brand names in constantly throughout your conversation! It's called writing.

TH

Learning the Names of Trees

Today we seem happy to pollute our brains with the love lives of mediocre celebrities, obscure TV show plotlines, and the latest whims of fashion to emerge from a select group of people renowned for looking utterly ridiculous themselves. All this pointless information is pushing out the knowledge passed down over generations about the real world around us. Take, for example, the humble tree. I bet you can identify more of Kylie Minogue's previous boyfriends and films starring Johnny Depp than you can native American trees. How many trees do you know? Be honest—four, five? Perhaps the oak, elm, pine, willow, and the maple. But what about the walnut, the ash, birch, wild cherry, English elm, hawthorn, hazel, juniper, hornbeam, yew, aspen, poplar, cypress, myrtle, or redbud tree? Then there's the spruce pine, sycamore, sweet gum, Texas persimmon, larch, and on and on and on it goes. Reclaim your brain, and learn the names of trees.

DK

Writing a Letter

To sit at a computer-free desk with a fountain pen, to pull out a sheet of your hand-printed headed notepaper, to write those first two words "Dear Friend," and then to pause awhile before letting the ink flow onto the page with tales of your doings and your worries, to fold up the paper, slip it into an envelope, write the address out, stick on the stamp, drop it into the mailbox, and then to imagine the pleasure that your letter will bring, the physical pleasure of opening it and reading it at the other end — ah, is this not happiness?

TH

Jumping for Joy

Just out of pure joy of being in the world, sometimes you want to leap in the air and click your
feet together, like the tumblers, troubadours,
and jesters of old. Jumping for joy is a pointless
act and should be indulged for that very reason.

TH

Hugs

The hug. Nature's very own antidepressant.
Scientists will tell you that hugs reduce blood
pressure, but everyone knows a warm, generous
hug can lift you out of the darkest gloom. Hugs
tear away the scaffolding of self-importance we
erect around ourselves—sidestepping pretension
to get into the center of a warmer inner whole.
Fears of impending doom vanish in the swoop
of a lover's arms. Hugs release tension, give you
strength, and help you face the unknown.

DK

Wandering around Old Churches

Despite the best efforts of the Puritans in reformed countries to ransack their treasures, there are still wonders to be seen and magical stories to be gleaned from old churches. Wooden carvings bear testament to the woodcarver's skill. Imagine also the patience and artistry of those who chiseled the letters in the gravestones. In some churches imps and gargoyles can be found, and intricately decorated fonts. Most churches are still — quite wonderfully — unlocked, so can be visited at any time of day as a refuge from the busy honking world outside. Eat your lunchtime sandwiches there, nap on the pews, sit and stare for as long as you can.

TH

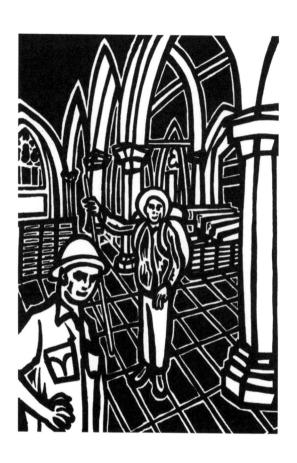

Shadow Watching

Shadows are where bad people lurk. We're told we're hiding in the shadow of others if we don't "achieve" as much as we should. But shadows are the essence of something far more meaningful than a reflection of physical form. Shadows are the corners of our mind the light of reason rarely touches. They offer a window into another world: the world of eternal darkness that all too many of us love to fear. It was the Chinese Han dynasty that gave us shadow puppets. One of Emperor Wu of Han's concubines died and he was so stricken with grief that he ordered his servants to raise her from the dead, and so, with a lamp and a figure made of donkey leather, they brought her shadow back to life. Things turn even more eerie when it comes to shadow people. These are dark figures that are said to inhabit our peripheral vision (accompanied by a feeling of terrible dread), only to vanish if you try to look at them directly. But these metaphors of fear hide a much more relaxing and wonderful truth. Those dark corners of the mind are not full of fear and woe, but are the first steps on the path of truth.

DK

The Garden Shed

The humble garden shed, preferably self-built, is man's free space. It offers endless opportunities for useless dawdling, pointless puttering, and fruitless frittering about. The shed is both a retreat and a canvas on which to arrange your jam jars, unfinished carpentry projects, and half-empty paint cans. In the shed you can dump anything that it seems a shame to throw away but for which you cannot find a use. In the shed you can sit on the old beaten-up armchair and relax in surroundings that remain blissfully free of a makeover inspired by an interior design magazine. In the shed you can dream up crazy schemes and stare at the wall, alone and at peace. A shed is a temple of uselessness, and what could be more noble than that?

TH

Sit-Ins

"Sit down for your rights!" proclaim
revolutionaries of a more lackadaisical
persuasion. Sit-ins are doubly effective because
doing nothing itself is an act of rebellion in
these work/haste-obsessed times. It is more
gentlemanly to sit lazily beneath your placard,
perhaps drinking a cup of coffee, than marching
and shouting.

DK

The Contemplation of Things That Fly

Because we can't fly we are fascinated by the sight of things that can. I have always loved watching things that appear to be weightless in the air, not just birds and insects, but floating thistledown, autumn leaves, scraps of wind-blown paper, clouds, balloons, and bubbles. Airborne creatures had the same kind of appeal to each of my children. Even when they were babies, lying in their stroller, they were very quick to notice a bee or a butterfly or a passing bird, and their suddenly focused eyes would search for whatever it was a long time after it had flown out of sight. When they were older, say, three or four, they tried to emulate the birds by holding bunches of feathers, flapping their arms, and jumping up in the air; and a few years later they copied them again by making paper planes in their image and tossing them off the hill behind our house. If one of these caught an updraft and floated away over the trees, there was huge excitement, as if a bird's own magic had got into it. Then the children would flap their arms again and run, leaping, down the hill.

CY

109

Squeezing Bubble Wrap

Oh, Bubble Wrap, how can I pop thee? Let me count the ways . . .

1. Idly during a conversation you'd rather not be entangled in.

2. With a toddler. Watch its face digest the unfathomable delights of being able to make something go *pop*.

3. On realizing mournfully how crappy the new gadget you bought for hundreds of dollars that was wrapped up in the Bubble Wrap actually turned out to be.

4. Scrunching up a huge piece in a tight ball to make the sound of a machine gun.

5. By using it as a no-frills sleeping bag. Bubble Wrap offers insulation from the cold at a fraction of the cost of the normal camping variety. It would be perfect, if the moment you rolled over you didn't wake everyone else up with a POP! POP! POP!

DK & GR

Whistling

Do you remember how beautifully your grand-father would whistle? Those trills, those melodic runs, that richness, that volume, that assurance? We need to practice our whistling, our ability to make music with the body by relying on nothing outside of ourselves for tunes and merriment. Whistling can change your mood and lift the spirits of those around you. Whistling can be jolly or mournful. But it needs practice. The more you do it, the better you will get, so whistle all day long, in the elevator, in the train, in the car, in the sandwich bar. Be bold, make some noise!

TH

Morning Sex

Unlike the frantic performance sex that descends after a night on the town, morning sex is deliciously unpretentious, relaxing, and slow. With the dust of sleep still in your eyes, an arching back, and a contented and effortless giggle, you toy with your lover. Gathering him or her in, as your ankles and buttocks writhe together under the sheets. Producing a grin on your lover's face before the new light of day has even touched his or her eyes.

Afterward you join the sun of a Saturday morning with a tranquil, satisfied relish. A tray of toasted muffins appears along with a pot of coffee. If there's a more perfect way to start the day, I haven't discovered it yet.

DK

Getting Dressed

Take some time in the evening to think about tomorrow's clothes in a relaxed frame of mind, in the bath, over a glass of wine perhaps. Ponder your options; relish turning the different colors, shapes, layers, over in your mind with full reference to the given season. Mentally select items and assemble them in your mind's eye.

When you've a model of what it is you're going to be wearing, don't wait until the morning; put your clothes out in the evening. Handle them with a certain degree of occasion, of ritual, and enjoy thinking ahead to the moment of actually wearing them.

You see, the following morning when you're all bleary-eyed and the psychic sluice gate opens and floods the gray matter with questions and fear, you can cut right through all that and be comforted, cradled, by the warm fibrous extension of your living self. Having your clothes ready to slip into in the morning isn't one less thing to worry about; it's one more thing to enjoy. Go on, check yourself in the mirror for a minute longer. Yes, indeed. You look great.

JD

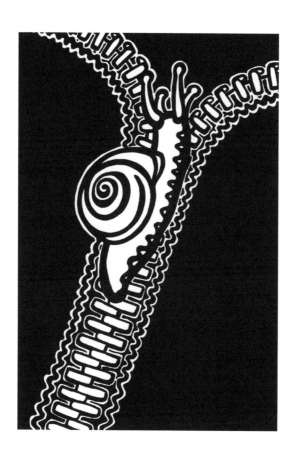

117

Smiling

It's interesting that we smile when we're happy but also when we're anxious and afraid. We revel in our smiles when laughter descends and pull them out of the psychological drawer to fend off anxiety or if there's no one around to give us a much-needed hug. This makes the smile a Darwinian arrow of optimism through the DNA of humanity. Smiling is all there is left when your breath finally leaks away.

DK

119

Breast-Feeding

Your task is to sit for hours, stare out of a
window, listen to the birds, and watch the
dawn, the sunset, the blossoms, or the rain.
Around you others clean and tidy and cook. You
cuddle a tiny creature, gaze at it, test the silki-
ness of its ear, rest your finger on a satin cheek,
and trace the line of its eyebrow. You are in
no doubt that this is the most important job in
the world. And it produces drugs: cozy, happy,
warming endorphins that silence the mutterings
of your intellect and your worries, and shut out
the mad fury of the world. You might listen to
NPR at three a.m., discuss a jigsaw puzzle at
nine a.m., instruct the father how to cook
Bolognese sauce at five p.m. Or you might lie
back on your feathered pillows and zone out of
everyday life.

VH

Libraries

Unfairly maligned as being either too old and scruffy or too modern and clinical — public libraries all have one thing in common. Their shelves are rammed with doorways to worlds you can peer through for free. These wormholes will take you to the inner workings of the political class in ancient Greece, the risqué pictures of photography manuals, love lives of the people in Victorian stately homes, quantum mechanics, the gardens of Japan, making catapults, the sexual antics of drug-addled rock stars, iguanodons, dictionaries full of exciting new swearwords, the mind of Richard Brautigan — the list is literally endless! Then, of course, there's the cheery old lady in a cardigan who smiles politely every time you pop in but you're convinced she knows all there is to know about the Marquis de Sade. Libraries are time capsules. Full of everything you could wish to know or understand all encased in the kind of shell that seems so utterly devoid of excitement you must have a secret password in order for your brain to want to gain entry. That password is a combination of curiosity and free time.

DK

Forgetting

Sometimes we need to release our mental burden and just say to ourselves: forget it. Let all the memories, good or bad, gently flow out of our consciousness. "To close the doors and windows of consciousness for a time," wrote Nietzsche. "To remain undisturbed by the noise of utility organs working with and against one another ... to make room for new things ... that is the purpose of active forgetfulness, which is like a doorkeeper, a preserver of psychic order, repose and etiquette." Furthermore, said Nietzsche of this important pleasure: "it will be immediately obvious how there could be no happiness, no cheerfulness, no hope, no pride, no present, without forgetfulness."

TH

Doodling

Pens live under their own unknowable laws.
They appear, chewed and topless, in the
unlikeliest places or collect all together in
unknown drawers. Once snared, a pen may be
reticent to let you draw its ink into the outside
world. Circles get it going on a scrap of paper,
but before you know it, you've forgotten what
you wanted it for and it's using you to unleash
its doodle. Perhaps this time I'll magically draw
something brilliant, you think to yourself; oh,
no, just another meaningless doodle. What did
I want to write down on my shopping list? Oh,
no! Another doodle! The doodle is the soul of
an idle pen. Yes, it could be used excitedly to
write a masterpiece or grudgingly to compare
mortgages and interest rates, but so much better
to unleash its doodle. The doodle is the hand and
the mind going out on an idle ramble. You can
doodle everywhere, the front of old envelopes,
that solitary last Post-it note and the back of
yesterday's torn-off calendar page. Doodles
everywhere!

DK

Slippers

In the days of the go-getting trainer, the humble slipper is a forgotten pleasure. Once upon a time, we would return home after a day of toil and remove our work boots and symbolically cast off the workaday world and instead put on our slippers, that symbol of warm domestic coziness, those comforters for the feet, the wearing of which will prevent you from doing any work. Certainly it is impossible to run while wearing slippers. Now the boot and the slipper have merged together into a single unit — the trainer — and the pleasure of the contrast is forgotten.

TH

Yawning

Deliciously contagious but hard to repress in the company of a tedious bore, yawning is nature's way of persuading you to take a break. Close your eyes, sit back, and relax as the sensation of sloth envelops your mouth. Inhale luxuriously through your nose as your eyes lightly water and then revel in your impending triumph. Growl out your yawn like a sated lion in the evening sun.

DK

Fishing

Fishing is meditation for Everyman. It is a kind of excusable idleness. You are doing nothing and doing something at the same time. Angling harmonizes activity and inactivity. It offers us the chance to sit and gaze at nature, at the water, to use our senses. When fishing, we see, we hear, we smell more intensely than in the workaday world. The pleasures of drinking coffee or eating a sandwich are somehow intensified on the riverbank. And if you do happen to catch a fish, then that is an additional bonus. But if you're an idler, then it's certainly not the point.

TH

Pacing

Pacing gets your brain juices going. While pondering a problem or working out an argument in your head, it's best to pace around. The great Mr. Lazy may have said, "Never run when you can walk, never walk when you can sit down, and never sit down when you can lie down," but pacing is far more half-hearted than it sounds. This is not the stomping march of a frustrated salesman, but the languid stroll giving you a guided tour of your home. You can float around the room in circles or dive off down the hall as you wrestle with a cumbersome idea. Pacing is the lazy and thinking person's friend. It cajoles you into thought, makes mincemeat of quandaries, and soon pulls full-blown ideas and theories from your stagnant head. It wakes you up when you're half asleep but doesn't take you anywhere that might prove to be too dangerous. In the kitchen to the kettle perhaps, before making a cup of tea, or while hanging up some damp pants and emptying the washing machine.

DK

Skipping Stones

Completely free and always enjoyable, skipping stones connects us with the water and the infinite yonder. Will you aim for five little bounces or two huge ones? Which stones skip the best? Who can get the stone farthest out to sea? Can anyone reach the opposite bank of the pond? Then there is the pleasurable search for the perfectly smooth stone: not too small, not too heavy, but as flat as possible for maximum "skippage." Compare, if you dare, the physical pleasure and connection with nature offered by stone skipping with the boredom and uniformity and expense of digital amusements.

TH

Merrymaking

The best nights out aren't planned. They are the nights when everything just seems to fall into place. The nights when you only popped out for a quick one and ended up stumbling home in the grip of hilarity with a new best friend as dawn rises over the river. It's hard to believe it could be time for work again in just a few hours. The night is lost in jokes and shenanigans, unusual drinks, and the soundtrack of the music of chance. Coincidence and serendipity are always the best guides. Once out and about you're equipped to recognize the possibilities of the night and the people around you, leading you to nooks and crannies of the town you could never have imagined visiting: strange bars, basement clubs, and forgotten town squares. You and the cats are winding your way home now. Past the whistling street cleaners, night buses, and postmen. You greet your front door with a grin, and marvel at how relaxed and sober you suddenly feel. Just time for a few cups of coffee and then you'll be back out to the office again.

DK

Lying Around in Fields

Doing nothing might just save the planet. When you lie in a field, you reconnect with the earth without harming it. If everyone had lain around in fields for the last two hundred years, rather than building factories, cars, guns, and airplanes, there would have been a lot less death and a lot less environmental damage. The way to save the planet is to refrain from attacking it, and therefore lying on it peacefully is a radical act of healing.

TH

Watching the River Flow

Standing on a bridge, watching the river flow
below, has always been a favorite pastime of
mine. Brought up, as I was, on the banks of the
River Esk in Musselburgh, I would often tarry
awhile on the Old Roman Bridge, scoffing a
hot meat pie from the adjacent baker's, when
I should have been rushing between the annex
and the main school building. Swans and ducks
would supply diversion and one could also spot
sticklebacks and other small fish darting hither
and thither in the smooth-flowing waters below.
Mirth was occasionally provided on hot days
when mill workers or drunks from the nearby
Brig Tavern ventured in for a paddle, a cheer
going up when an unsteady wader lost his foot-
ing on the rocky riverbed. I would toss the last
fragment of my piecrust to the ducks and then
head off back to school, late for my next lesson,
fortified by my stolen moments on the bridge.

JS

Butterfly Hunting

"My pleasures are the most intense known to man," wrote the trilingual tennis player and writer Vladimir Nabokov, "writing and butterfly hunting." Tripping down the country lanes, wondering at the fragility and beauty of the painted ladies and monarchs and red admirals, is a profoundly enjoyable pursuit. So go get a net and get out into the wilds, or simply observe those delicate decorated wisps of nothing as they flutter by.

TH

Hiding

When life gets too much, don't fall for the doctor's potions and pills that conspire with your body to get you straight back to work. Have the confidence to listen to yourself when you can feel that something is wrong. It's not you that's wrong. You're having an entirely reasonable reaction to the chaos of the modern world. There's nothing wrong with having enough of chaos every now and then.

Put a "Do Not Disturb" sign up outside your front door, ignore the phone when it rings, turn off the computer so you can't "get mail," switch your cell phone to silent and fling it into the bottom of an old drawer, forget about the newspaper, unplug the TV, leave all the chores for tomorrow, and make a pot of tea.

DK

Cloud Watching

When we pause to look up from our earthbound
scurrying, we will see that the skies offer an
ever-changing drama. Clouds shift and flow and
move: the sky is never the same two seconds in
a row. As the sun moves, so the colors change,
and the interplay between the wind, the temper-
ature, and the sun creates spectacles of infinite
variety. Clouds will form themselves into
fantastic shapes, even for a second appearing to
resemble an object from our world: a donkey,
a tortoise, or a saucepan. Then they are gone,
ever-changing, formless yet with form, solid yet
fluid at once.

TH

149

Snow

It's early. The moon and the stars are giving way
to the faint warming of dawn as you close the
door and creep carefully outside, hoping not
to break the spell. Your boots crunch the perfect snow that's still falling, carefully layering
itself methodically over every scrap of the path
up ahead. The park beckons. Ahead of you the
murky grip of night is handing the baton to a
safer world of childhood glee. The world feels
empty but certainly not afraid. There is a hush
and tranquillity.

DK

Arranging Flowers

Of all the domestic arts, picking flowers from the garden or hedgerow or field or wood and then arranging them in a vase before putting the vase in the window is surely one of the most exquisite of idle pleasures. The timeless act of cutting the flowers and then placing them together in the vase encourages you to look closely at the miracle of the petals and the colors and the leaves, and to notice that every flower is slightly different from the other. There are never two the same. Is it not wondrous to reflect on the magic of nature's very own dawdling firework display as the tiny seed grows in dirt over months to produce these random and colorful parades?

TH

Thrift Shop ESP

Seek out a thrift shop and, before you push open the badly painted door and hear the tinny little bell, think of an author or a book you've always meant to read but, for some reason or other, have never got around to getting. Visualize them, or it, in your mind and then stride purposefully through the door, beyond the slightly musty-smelling clothes, the sad and rejected shelf of toys, and stop confidently in front of the overly laden bookshelves. Even if they don't have the book or the author you want, there is bound to be something that catches your eye. Thrift shops' bookshelves are rarely arranged in alphabetical order, which makes them brilliant for stumbling through. They are a muddled-up jigsaw of books instead, made up from the bookshelves of the recently dead.

DK

Leaning on Gates

There's nothing so free and easy as leaning on
gates. The five-bar gate has its top bar positioned
at the perfect height for a good lean. From the
gate, you can lean and slouch and quietly watch
busy nature bustling around you. You can smile
and ponder and think. The trick is to put one
foot up on the lowest rung of the gate. This
gives you a certain necessary level of commit-
ment to the act of leaning. Without the foot on
the bottom bar, the leaning is too temporary. In
this position you can lean comfortably for anywhere up to half an hour.

TH

Overnight Trains

Slow travel is when the journey isn't seen as a chore but a reason for going somewhere in itself. The perfect example of this is an overnight train. Taking your time to get somewhere allows you to acclimatize to your destination and gives you a proper travel experience. You can stare out of the window once you've chucked your BlackBerry out of it, and leave your laptop at home while you're at it. Trains have huge panoramic windows, so you can idly stare out of them. Enjoy the chance to do absolutely nothing for once. Allow your thoughts to meander through special memories you rarely seem to have the time to reach. Philosophize at will, pondering loves and remembering times of laughter with favorite friends. The train dawdles along the track, offering ever-changing vistas and characters for your curiosity to navigate. Breathe in and out slowly, marveling at how sedate and unstressful travel can become, but only if you release the time to devote to it.

DK

Whittling

Unleash your creativity with the simple act of whittling away at a stick with your penknife. Marvel at the satisfaction as, through your own efforts, the stick starts to become a work of art before your very eyes, to turn magically from a mere twig into an object of beauty, uniquely expressive of you. Marvel at the wonders that can happen when man and nature work in harmony, and compare that life-affirming process to the dead glow of Photoshop and PowerPoint.

TH

Watching Hail Bounce Off the Pavement

Occasionally the gods like to put us in our place by reminding us of the power of the natural world. A kind of natural therapy, it reminds us of what is important and how insignificant we all are. What our ancestors made of the great hunks of ice when they crashed to earth in thousands of balls, we can only guess. Armed with scientific knowledge, we can put fear to one side and gasp instead at the power of these pebbles of ice that up till now were violently rattling in the clouds high above our head. They clatter on the roof of cars and turn the pavements into a firing range, leaving anguished pedestrians fumbling for their keys in haste. Occasionally they threaten to shatter your windows that are so steamed up from your excited breath that you have to wipe them feverishly just to watch the progress of these mighty frozen stones. Nervousness gives way to glee and you urge them on with their wanton destruction as they attempt to cleanse the tired and grimy earth.

DK

Stargazing

Lying there on the roof of your car pondering the eternal mysteries of the universe, and thanking God that you are not Richard Dawkins, is surely one of the most ancient and readily available pleasures in the natural world. Just what the hell are those twinkly things? Do they even still exist? Gazing at the stars is a pleasure available to everyone, even if you are "in populous city pent," as Coleridge put it. Despite the best attempts of scientists to explain the universe, gazing at the stars will still fill us with wonder and sweet delicious confusion.

TH

Watching the Birds

Oh, to lie in a field and simply gaze up at passing birds, as I did, and probably you did, too, that time before we could even pronounce our own name. Buzzards are, in my opinion, the best birds to concentrate on, as they seem to actually enjoy just hanging around at very high altitudes, especially on a clear spring day when they weave endlessly about looking for a mate. Last April I spent a very happy afternoon lying motionless in the grass, watching three different buzzards as they soared and seemed to hover high above me. They were so high, in fact, that I needed binoculars to confirm that they really were birds and not tiny motes floating in the surface of my eyes. I watched them swooping, looping, and sailing upward again for hours, and when I finally walked home, I felt as light as paper. If only I'd remembered to flap my arms, I'm sure I would have risen a few feet into the air.

CY

Gossip

Chitchatting away about the doings of our neighbors and friends is a delightful distraction from taking a cold, hard look at our own problems. Really? Well, I never. I always thought they were so happy. Has he? Oh, poor dear. I don't want to take sides, but he was rather too fond of the ladies. I don't know how she put up with it. It's like a soap opera around here, we say, and realize that we don't need a soap opera for the simple reason that we have one "around here."

TH

Leaning on Walls

Unlike park benches, walls are everywhere; but just like park benches, they give you the chance to rest. Take a moment to watch the world go by from your temporary vantage point. Lean on your own and you may begin to feel self-conscious, but with a prop you'll be able to remain leaning for some time. A squashed and folded paperback book is perfect, but avoid newspapers at all costs. Quite apart from filling you with trivial nonsense, they flap irritatingly, becoming unreadable, in even the slightest breeze. So take a breather, and read one more chapter, before plodding off on your way to the park.

DK

Grooming

A little trimming, a little slicking back, a little perfuming, a little ruffling, and a little gazing in the mirror. Brush your hair or brush someone else's hair. Make braids, create parts, tie up bunches. Grooming is the art of practicing creativity on your own body. Even some picking of the nose or scouring of the ears. Some little readjustments in the bathroom, a dab of potions and lotions. Always a treat.

TH

Philosophizing

Sometimes you have to talk to find out what
you think.

DK

Straw Chewing

As an aid to contemplation, turning a bit of grass around between your teeth has yet to be improved by anything that the world of commodified pleasures has to offer. Just pluck a piece of flowering grass from the meadow or from the wasteland by the train tracks, and chew and ponder. It's an instinctive pleasure, and a simple act that will transform you into a Huckleberry Finn–*esque* loafer, a Walt Whitman, a Thoreau, drawing nutrients from the plant and enjoying the moment, free of care. Combine straw chewing with gazing off into the distance, shaking your head sagely, and grinning with all the wisdom of a Taoist monk, and you may well be on the road to enlightenment.

TH

Good Company

The evening closes in on a warm summer's day.
The wine is coursing through you and through
your friends, but not down into the tributary of
political discourse that can end up in an almighty
brawl, but down the waterfalls of laughing
memory. Long-forgotten stories and cackles
emerge of times past while grand plans are made
for the future still to be lived. Sharing bread,
barbecues, and those generous anecdotes — the
simple gentleness of caring for the people you
love.

DK

Building Houses of Cards

Wholly without use, the house of cards is frag-
ile, difficult, and supremely satisfying. It is like
building your own little cathedral on the kitchen
table. And a mere breath or the lightest brush
of the sleeve can bring the whole lot crashing
down, reminding us of the temporary nature of
man's earthly creations and the vanity of human
wishes.

TH

Cycling

Cycling is possibly the greatest and most pleasurable form of transport ever invented. It's like walking, only with one-tenth of the effort. Ride through a city and you can understand its geography in a way that no motorist, contained by one-way signs and traffic jams, will ever be able to. You can whiz from one side to the other in minutes. You can overtake $250,000 sports cars that are going nowhere fast. You can park pretty much anywhere. It truly is one of the greatest feelings of freedom one can have in a metropolitan environment. It's amazing you can feel this free in a modern city — one day they'll work out a way to tax and bureaucratize any fun out of it. Luckily, they haven't. Yet. So enjoy it while you can — nothing this good ever seems to last forever.

DP

Dancing

Alas, for many of us, dancing is only indulged in at weddings after having consumed large quantities of alcohol, enough to throw off one's inhibitions and move one's body roughly in time with the music. This, of course, is a great shame. Not so long ago, we used to dance every night after dinner. Dancing masters were frequent visitors to the home. Dancing is pure fun and escapism: when we are whirling dervishes, we forget about our worries and our strife. Dancing can also be a prelude to sex and can remind us that life is to be lived and enjoyed. Merriment, festivity, and ritual have all but vanished from our lives. Let us bring them back.

TH

Reading Edward Lear Poems Out Loud to Children

Admittedly, this pleasure is not necessarily free, as you might have to buy Lear's *A Book of Bosh* in the first place. But you can pick it up in the used book shop, or indeed borrow it from the library and copy the poems out by hand. You'll then have a storehouse of treasures forever. Start by reading "The Owl and the Pussycat" and then move on to "The Pobble Who Had No Toes," "The Jumblies," and "The Dong with a Luminous Nose." Watch their big round eyes stare at you as you read. Leave gaps so they can recite:

> *Far and few, far and few,*
> *Are the lands where the Jumblies live.*
> *Their heads are green and their hands are blue*
> *And they went to sea in a sieve.*

A gentle genius, Lear was one of twenty-two children, a fact that seems to fascinate all kids. Lear poems are concerned with loss, yearning, and the desire to run away to a magical land, and so are just as satisfying for adults as for little ones.

TH

Laundromats

The enormous laundry bag is designed for crew members on a round-the-world yacht race, but it can't seem to cope with all your shirts and pants. An almighty effort raises it to your shoulder and you lurch down the street to the Laundromat. You open the door and the warmth hits you. The lady with a kind smile that hides bad teeth shuffles up and down looking for an empty machine. She finds one and gestures for you. That single machine swallows all your clothes in one go. In goes the powder; you add the coins and watch your undies begin to roll slowly over and over in the slushy white foam.

That book you've been reading is more tempting than the gossip pages of a tabloid, but still you flick through the paper, tutting quietly to yourself, before reclining in the pages of your book. Ah, the bliss of forced idleness.

An hour later, everything is done. You feel slightly deflated that you have to leave your cozy refuge for another week so soon. But the bag feels lighter and the warmth of your clothes nuzzles your shoulder on the way home.

DK

Choosing to Get Wet in the Rain

We create ourselves a lot of needless fuss and bother by huffing and puffing and trying to keep dry during a rainstorm. How liberating it is to abandon all ideas of dryness and give yourself up to the downpour. Don't run, stroll. Look up, smile, and enjoy the sensation of water from the heavens refreshing your careworn face. The wetter you get, the more free you will feel. Once you're inside and standing, dripping, on your mat at home, the laughter will begin to take hold. You remove your sodden, wet suit and make a dash for the bathroom (so much the better if you don't happen to be on your own). Every inch of you is utterly drenched as huge great globules of water dribble down your nose. Dry yourself off, wrap yourself in a robe, and devour a pack of cookies on the sofa with a cup of hot chocolate.

TH

Reading Gravestones

I was early for a wedding once. I began to amble through the graveyard. The names of the dead drifted past me. I went deeper and deeper until one particular double grave made me stop. It was like a raised flowerbed with a single broad stone headboard across its top edge. The grave itself was just a rough surface with an empty granite vase in the middle.

Engraved upon the left of the broad stone were the words:

Wing Commander Andrew Phillips
Born April 3rd 1918
Lost over France June 7th 1940
Loving husband of Connie

On the right, it said,

Connie Phillips
Born May 7th 1920
Died November 17th 2002

There was something wonderful and heartbreaking about the fact that she never remarried after losing her twenty-two-year-old husband when she was only just twenty herself. It conjured up scenes of Britain during the Second World War. Thoughts of the brief snatches of happiness these two people managed together. Of her six decades of grief when he was lost, perhaps flying a Spitfire as one of Churchill's "few." You can imagine her waiting, hoping against hope that one day he might return.

But then I realized that her remains were alone under that stone she'd tended so lovingly for so long, while his were buried in some unmarked field in the French countryside, and broke completely. Despite the tears on my cheeks, my shoulders felt broader as I made my way back to the church. I found myself smiling that their story could be stumbled upon, and move to tears a complete stranger years and years later.

DK

Folding Paper

Whether you are folding up a letter to put into an envelope, folding a piece of paper to make a paper airplane, or folding a square piece of paper to make a water bomb or a playground fortune-teller, there is something infinitely satisfying at the effect that mere folding can have on a flat piece of nothing. Through the agency of no more than your hands, a blank sheet is transformed into an object of beauty or fun or utility, and you become, briefly, a craftsman at your desk. This is the beauty of origami: it's office-friendly and completely free.

TH

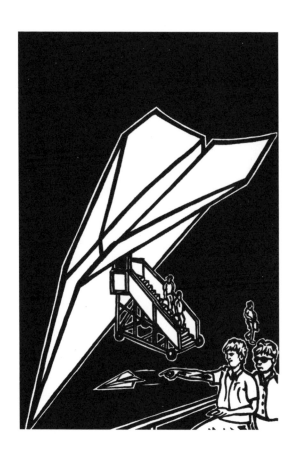

Feeding the Birds

While standing at the sink, your gaze wanders through the kitchen window and onto the bird feeder in the middle of the yard. Bits of chopped-up suet are being devoured by chattering finches. Sunflower seeds are attracting a whistling cardinal.

Birds are a gift, aren't they? They fly for you, sing for you, contort through the air and dance. All for the price of a few old scraps of food. Then there's the joy to be had in making a bird feeder. Make it tall enough and far enough away from a tree or a fence to dissuade prowling cats, not too spacious to invite intrusion from larger quarry, a basic roof to keep out the winter rain, and a small hook for a seed cake or two. Specific seed types attract different birds, but anything you have left over will probably be fine. The strobing flecks of yellow, blue, and green that hit your peripheral vision with every tiny wing beat are compliments to you. They snatch something and then vanish, only to reappear again and again and again. So keep it coming, especially in the cold, or your floating friends will take their fleeting show to another feeder, in another yard, leaving you and the dish washing alone.

DK

199

Bell Ringing

Bell ringing is properly called change ringing. Done correctly, it requires very little physical strength but offers a refreshing workout for the brain, as the whole point is to ring a series of sequences (or changes) on a set of bells with no repetition. There are thousands of tunes, or "methods," with wonderful names like Reverse Canterbury Pleasure and Grandsire Doubles, expressed as "blue line" diagrams to help the ringers navigate. Change ringing combines math, music, engineering, and the subversive pleasure of making a very loud noise in public. Plus, practice nights usually end up in the neighborhood pub. No wonder John Bunyan thought it an "odious vice" no better than dancing, playing dominoes, or reading historical romances.

JM

Lying in Hammocks

Few of mankind's inventions can trump the humble hammock. Originating, as you may imagine, in the Caribbean, the hammock is believed to have been invented by a lackadaisical fisherman who decided to turn his net to good use when he'd finished fishing for the day, hanging it between two trees to sleep in and thus avoiding the need to go home and hurry back to work the following morning. Raised from the ground he was safe from any nasty creepy-crawlies that might amble by during the night, not to mention an overzealous moonlit tide, and he got a good hour of extra sleep because he didn't have to do the coconut tree commute to get to his fishing boat the next morning.

The word *hammockable* (describing two trees that are the perfect distance apart between which a hammock can be hung) is not in the dictionary, but it should be. It is surely the laziest word ever written. I would start a campaign for it to be included in the next edition, but I can't tear myself away from the hammock I'm writing this from. So I think I'll sleep here in my clothes for a while instead. Good night.

DK

Contributors

TH Tom Hodgkinson

DK Dan Kieran

DP Daniel Pemberton

CY Chris Yates

JS Jock Scot

VH Victoria Hull

MDA Matthew De Abaitua

NL Nick Lezard

AM Andrew Male

JD Jamie Dwelly

JM John Mitchinson

MB Michael Bywater

IV Ian Vince